Modern Block Printing

Modern Block Printing

Over 15 projects designed
to be printed by hand

Rowan Sivyer

Hardie Grant

BOOKS

Contents

Introduction

Block printing is the art of transferring ink or paint onto paper or fabric, with either a carved block or a textured object. It is also known as relief printing. As opposed to etching (where ink is rubbed *into* the lines of an etching plate), or screen printing (where ink is pushed *through* the open parts of a screen), relief printing involves the ink being rolled *onto* the areas of the stamp that is not carved away and it is this 'relief' that is then printed onto the paper or fabric. Block printing is therefore the overall term for an art form that includes lino printing, woodcut printing and stamping, and printing with or without a press. Block printing can also include printing with objects that have a relief but that have not been carved, such as vegetables and fruit or household items.

Block printing is easy, fun and addictive. It is a great way to make marks and express yourself without worrying about your drawing skills (everything looks better printed), and a basic printing set-up is affordable and containable. It is also a versatile and transferable art form that you can use to enhance the other arts and crafts you might pursue. If you are into collage, block printing allows to make your own papers. If you love sewing, block printing gives you access to unique, custom-made fabrics. If you enjoy embroidery, block printing can add interest to your pieces. If you are into ceramics, consider the textures you can create with relief printing. The projects in this book are designed to get you thinking about the many ways in which you can use block printing, from wall art to homewares.

For myself, block printing is an art form that continues to challenge me creatively, while supporting my mental health. What do I mean by that? I believe that taking time to make with our hands helps us to slow down, to unplug, to focus on the doing. Carving by hand is a form of meditation for me. My breathing slows, my mind stills. My hands focus on cutting out bits of rubber, one piece at a time. Once the block is finished, my attention turns to printing it. The thrill of inking up a block for the first time and seeing how it prints. The joy of the reveal is tangible, and I never tire of it.

How to use this book

This book is designed to demystify block printing and provide tips, tricks and project ideas, both for those who are new to block printing and for people who have been doing it for a while. I truly believe this is an art form that is accessible to all ages and abilities.

The first section, like all arts and crafts books, discusses tools and materials. This is not an exhaustive list by any means, but rather a list of the things that have worked well for me and for my students in the past.

The second section goes on to look at the basics of stamp design, transferring, carving and printing, before exploring different techniques in relation to colour, masking and patterns. This section is designed to allow you to advance your block printing, to provide some inspiration as you experiment with this wonderful art form, and to help you with the projects.

Finally, **the last section** provides 17 projects designed to put your skills and techniques to the test. Although I provide some designs and templates, my ultimate desire is to see you run with these ideas and make them your own. Put your own stamp on it (pun definitely intended)!

A SIDE NOTE:

This book tends to focus on carving PVC rubber, as well as printing with non-carved objects, because these are the techniques I find to be easiest and most satisfying. The techniques and tools I use are, for the most part, transferable to linoleum and wood. Please feel free to experiment with whatever you have available, and try to find out what works for you. After all, it is through trying and doing that we learn the most.

Tools and materials

Easy-carve rubber

When it comes to carving materials, we have many choices from wood and vinyl, to linoleum (lino from now on) and soft-carve rubber. For this book and the projects within, I would recommend using soft-carve rubber – if soft-carve is not available, or your budget does not allow for it, then use lino. Carving wood can be tricky to master for most beginners (and for seasoned carvers as well).

Some rubbers are better than others; my rubber of choice is Renoir Ezy-Carve because of its thickness but I also really enjoy carving Speedball Speedy-Carve. Experiment with what is available and see which one works best for you.

 I often get asked by my students about my preference for PVC rubber over lino, and I give them several reasons:

1. *Rubber is easier and safer to carve.* Lino becomes increasingly hard and brittle the longer it sits on the shelf. You need to warm it as you go, and I often find I cannot control how much lino I am cutting. If your carving tools are not sharp enough, then you will find yourself pushing harder and sometimes your tool will skid across the lino... into your hand. Rubber/PVC rubber is softer to carve. I can carve for longer without strain to my wrist, and I don't have to put as much pressure on my tools so there is far less chance of an accident.

2. *Rubber is easier to print with.* PVC rubber is easy to pick up and print with without having to mount it. The thinness of lino means that you often need to mount it in order to block print with it, which just adds an extra step between carving the stamp and printing the stamp. PVC is also easier to cut down to size (no hessian backing getting in the way) and it doesn't curl when it gets wet.

3. *Rubber is more versatile when it comes to inking up.* I have used archival oil-based inkpads, relief printing ink, acrylic paint and screen printing inks on PVC rubber. Also, PVC rubber is not as 'thirsty' as lino. To get a good, solid print from lino, you need to prime the block by taking multiple prints, whereas I can get a good print the first time I use a rubber block.

This is not to say that easy-carve rubber does not have its drawbacks. It is a little more expensive than lino. It is also true that lino, which is made of linseed oil, cork dust, wood flour and pine resin, is more environmentally sustainable than PVC rubber, which is essentially a plastic. I personally counter this by using as much of my offcut rubber as possible. The larger offcuts can be turned into more stamps, while the tiny scraps and shavings can be used as filling – for things like stress balls, juggling balls, door stops or even soft toys. It's also worth noting that soft-cut rubbers come in set sizes, so if you want to create a print over 30 cm (12 in) high or wide, you may have to either use multiple pieces or turn to lino, which can come in rolls and be cut to size.

Carving tools

Carving tools (gouges, blades, cutters) can vary in terms of blade shape and quality, and come in different sizes and with different handle lengths. I mainly use the shorter palm tools, because I find they are easier to use than the longer-handled tools). In general, carving blades come as a V, a U or a knife. V-shaped and U-shaped blades can vary in width and depth.

When you are starting off, a basic set of either wooden-handled or plastic-handled tools is perfectly adequate. Your first set of tools may include three to five separate tools, or it might consist of one tool with interchangeable blades, such as the Speedball cutter. While the latter can be cost-effective, having to change blade heads can be fiddly and tiresome if you are carving often.

When it comes to carving tools, you really do get what you pay for, which is why I highly recommend spending a little more money on some quality palm tools. Pfeil and Flexcut tools are favourites. The handles are ergonomic, sitting very comfortably in the hand, and the steel is of a high quality and super sharp – they cut through rubber like a hot knife through butter. Flexcut's palm tools only come in sets (I particularly like their micro tool set), whereas Pfeil tools can be bought in a set or individually. While it is fun to have a variety of different sizes and shapes, most of my carving is done with three tools:

1. a 0.5 mm or 1 mm wide U-shaped or V-shaped carving tool for fine lines
2. a wide and shallow U-shaped tool for clearing larger sections of filler or background
3. a tool with a mid-range sized gouge to vary the cuts

Tracing paper

I use cheap tracing paper to trace and transfer my designs to rubber. You can use baking or parchment paper if tracing paper is not available.

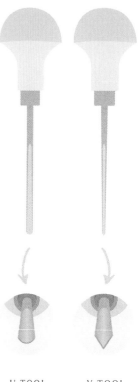

U TOOL   V TOOL

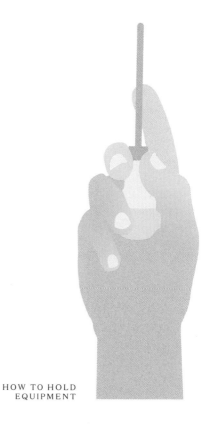

HOW TO HOLD
EQUIPMENT

Craft knife/X-acto blade/scalpel

A craft knife is very useful for cutting rubber blocks down to a manageable size and for trimming away excess rubber. An X-acto blade or a scalpel can also be used to cut into your stamp and carve pieces away.

Inkpads

If I am using smaller rubber blocks, or printing cards or testing colour ideas, I generally reach for an inkpad. Inkpads come in many different shapes and sizes. Larger inkpads cost more but last a long time, while smaller cubes or tear-shaped inkpads can be used to blend colours on a block itself. I prefer to work with archival oil-based pigment inks over water-based dye inkpads. I find that pigment inkpads sit on the PVC rubber blocks well whereas dye inks tend to puddle, leading to patchy prints. Some of my favourite brands of ink include Versafine, Versafine Clair, Delicata, Versacolor and Versamagic.

Block printing or relief ink

Relief inks can be water-based, oil-based or oil-based water-washable. The latter is my preferred type, because not only is the ink satisfyingly opaque and smooth, but it can also be washed off without the need for solvents. Ink comes in either tubes or tins, and a little goes a long way. You can also buy additives to mix with your relief inks: for example, you can buy extender, which helps to make the ink more transparent, or tack reducer to – you guessed it – reduce tack (stickiness). Relief ink stays 'open' for a long time, which means that if your printing is interrupted, you can return to it later and the ink will still be wet. However, this also means that prints take longer to dry. Just how long it takes can depend on the weather. Here in Sydney, where it is warm but often humid, it generally takes about three days for a print to dry. As with acrylic paints, block printing inks can be mixed to make the perfect colour for a project. I highly recommend spending a little time experimenting with mixing your inks and making test cards for future reference.

 ## Tool maintenance

If you have paid for good tools, you really should look after them! Make sure you store them safely. I use a leather tool pouch. Other people put corks on the end of their tools to protect the blades or find a rack-type solution.

As with kitchen knives, carving tools should be sharpened regularly; a sharp tool is a safe tool. You can sharpen your tools on a strop or a whetstone. A strop is a piece of leather that you rub with a honing or polishing compound before dragging your tool across the leather towards you repeatedly. A V-shaped tool is relatively straightforward to sharpen as long as you make the same number of strokes on each side. A U-shaped tool is harder to hone, so work in small sections around the curve. Once proficient, you can curl your tool while pulling it towards you, thus allowing the whole arc of the U to sharpen. Take note: the blade of a tool can be damaged through incorrect or over-vigorous honing, so take it slow and steady. A whetstone is a stone that has micro-abrasive particles that, when wet, works in a similar way to the strop.

When you sharpen your tools, a tiny metal burr may form on the inside of the tools. That's where a slipstone can come in handy. Flip your tool over and fit it over the top of the slipstone, then pull the tool towards you, thus removing the burr. Some strops come attached to a piece of wood that has different shaped ridges. These work in the same way as a slipstone, in that you pull the tool along them to remove the burr.

 How often you will need to sharpen your tools will depend on which material you are carving. If carving wood or lino, some printmakers recommend sharpening your tools every hour or so. Carving rubber requires less frequent sharpening, because the soft rubber does not dull the blade as quickly.

Inking plate

In order to roll out your relief ink, you need an inking plate. While you can buy specific inking plates from art stores, I use a large piece of thin acrylic, which is relatively cheap, light and cleans up easily.

Brayer

If you use block printing or relief ink, you need a brayer to roll out and apply the ink to your block. Brayers can be hard or soft and come in a range of widths from very thin 'editioning' brayers to super wide jumbo, double-handled brayers. I have a 5 cm (2 in), a 7 cm (2¾ in) and a 15 cm (6 in) brayer to do the bulk of my printmaking, although I also use a foam roller when rolling out screen printing ink. For consistent, even inking, it is good practice to use a brayer which is as wide as or wider than your block.

Acrylic paint

Using acrylic paint with your stamps is a great way of printing with what you already have, printing bold colours, printing over mediums that might resist oil-based inks, or printing something that you want to dry carefully. Heavy-body acrylics work better than fluid acrylics and you may want to use a brayer to roll the paint thinly. Keep in mind block printing with acrylic paint tends to be rustic-looking. Chunkier, simple blocks work better than those with a lot of detail because the paint tends to sink into the grooves. Acrylic paint tends to dry very quickly as it does not contain the retardants that relief printing inks do. You can increase the open time (the time that the paint stays wet and workable) by adding block printing medium.

Whatever paint you use, make sure you prioritise cleaning your stamps quickly because when acrylic dries it is difficult to remove and will fill the carved areas and possibly damage the surface of your stamp. I like to keep a container of water nearby when working with acrylic paint. As soon as I have finished with the stamp, I place it in the water until I have finished and am ready to clean up.

Fabric ink

For printing on fabric, the best option is a specific block printing ink for fabric. With the exception of Speedball Fabric Block Printing Ink, fabric inks will require some form of heat treatment (usually ironing) to set the ink on the fabric. I prefer Speedball Fabric Block Printing Ink because it comes in multiple colours, I can apply it to the block with my regular brayers and, once printed, the fabric can air-cure rather than requiring heat treatment to set the ink.

If I am printing fabric for a project that does not need to be laundered (perhaps a planter or a lampshade or a pouch), I like to use my regular relief ink because I enjoy having the colour options and the relief ink prints cleanly.

 If you have done any screen printing in your time, you may have left-over inks and you can use these to block print. Screen printing ink is generally more viscose than block printing inks and you may find that the ink can run into some of the grooves of your blocks. I like to let the ink sit out in the air for a little while before printing (which allows it to thicken) and I prefer to use a sponge roller to roll the ink onto the block.

Baren/spoon (and a note about presses)

If you have a large block and you intend to pull a print rather than stamp a print (understand the difference on page 30), then you may need something to help you 'burnish' your print – i.e. rub the paper to make sure all the ink transfers from the block to the paper. A baren is a disc-like tool with a flat, smooth bottom and a handle to allow you to apply even pressure. You can get barens made of wood, bamboo, metal or glass. My favourite baren is a metal spoon!

Even very large prints can be burnished by hand but when you are doing a lot of printing, it can be tough on the body. Many printmakers will opt for a press once they have been printing for a while, whether this is an etching press, a book press or a hand-lever press. Given the significant cost (both in money and space), I would emphasise that a press is a nice-to-have rather than a must-have for block printing.

Printmaking substrates

Paper

When you first start out in block printing you may find that paper is a little bit of an afterthought: after all, in reality you can print onto just about any kind of paper – and I should know, having printed on tissue, butcher's paper, recycled paper bags, newspaper, book paper, deli paper and so on. Beginning with copy paper and pre-scored cards is a great way to go.

If you choose to delve a little deeper into your local art store, you might find yourself in front of the paper racks where there will be over a dozen papers recommended for 'printmaking'. Paper varies in weight and texture and can enhance or limit your printmaking, so it pays to know which papers are better suited to printmaking techniques. With regards to block printing, heavy papers are better to use when printing with an etching press. For hand burnishing, thinner papers (120 gsm and below) are more suitable. I particularly like Japanese papers (hosho, kitakata and shirakaba), which are very thin but strong. Mulberry, banana and handmade papers can add to the feel of a particular piece; however, these papers can be quite textured and can be challenging to print on. When stamping, I prefer to use uncoated, smooth paper or cardstock.

Fabric

There are multiple projects in this book that involve printing on fabric, but which fabric is best? I find the fabrics that give me the best results are those that are closely woven, without much texture – cotton, linen, canvas, calico, denim, etc. Like with paper, it can really help to do your homework before you invest in large quantities of fabric. Get small swatches of multiple fabrics and test how they print. Does the print look faint or inconsistent? Does the ink soak through to your surface below? If it is dark fabric, does your ink show up on it? Once you have bought your fabric of choice, prepare it for printing by washing it to remove any sizing. I once painstakingly printed 3 metres (3⅜ yards) of calico as a table cover for a trestle table to use at markets. I sewed it all up and it fit perfectly – but the first time I put it in the wash it shrank! So, if you don't want any nasty surprises, don't neglect this step. Finally, remember to press your fabric prior to printing to make sure you have as smooth a print surface as possible – a stray crease can affect your print quality.

Techniques

Block printing without carving

If the idea of carving a motif feels intimidating, then you will be relieved to know you can block print with all sorts of things that you may already have in the house.

Printing with vegetables

Veg and fruit printing can be messy, but it is a great way to introduce kids to block printing. It is interesting to see the various shapes that different vegetables can make. When cut, the bottom of a bunch of celery or pak choi (bok choy) prints a convincing rose, while a single stick produces a crescent. Oranges and lemons (which you can print either pre- or post-juicing) produce spoked wheels. An apple cut in half prints a shape resembling a butterfly (depending on the variety, of course). A slice of star fruit produces ... you guessed it, star prints. A corn cob makes for interesting texture printing. Potatoes, carrots and sweet potatoes can be cut into shapes with a knife or even a cookie cutter. A slice of okra prints sweet little star-shaped florals. I even know of someone who has printed with a banana peel! Always try to dry the surface of the vegetable or fruit before printing with it. Roll out your ink or paint and stamp your cut vegetables into the ink before printing on paper or fabric.

Printing with found objects

If you would prefer to eat your greens rather than print with them, then go hunting around the house for other objects to print with. You would be surprised just what makes a pleasing block. In the Party Polka Dots! project on page 82, I use a selection of objects that give me different-sized spots, such as wine and Champagne corks, a pencil eraser and a cardboard inner tube. However, there are many other interesting things to print with if you just use your imagination. Raid your recycling bin and find some plastic bottles – use the caps or ink up the bottoms of the bottles. Do you have any old toy cars or stray pieces of Lego? How about wrapping some string or rubber bands around an unused wooden building block and then seeing how it prints? Try inking up some scissors. If you can find old pieces of pressed glass at thrift store, the bottoms make beautiful intricate prints.

Foam stamps

Craft foam stamps are fun to make and an inexpensive and easy way to start block printing. Some craft stores sell adhesive-backed foam, which makes it very simple: just cut out the shapes and stick the foam on to sturdy pieces of cardboard. For an even easier option, it is possible to buy pre-cut sticky-backed foam shapes. If you are cutting your own stamps, I recommend going for simple shapes – arches, triangles, circles, diamonds and rectangles all work well. You can also use a ballpoint pen or a skewer to etch simple designs into the foam. Making print blocks with foam is addictive – it is impossible to stop at one. Once you're happy with your shapes, print them with acrylic paint or block printing inks. At a pinch, you can create basic stamps out of styrofoam trays for you want a fun recycling project.

Basic stamp carving

Designing a simple stamp

While we have already seen that it is fun to block print with vegetables, foam and found objects, there is another level of satisfaction that comes from carving your own blocks or stamps. Any pencil drawing can become a stamp, but when it comes to designing your first stamp, there are a few key things to keep in mind.

1. Remember that whatever gets carved away becomes the white of the paper and whatever remains (the relief) is what will get printed. This is easy to understand on paper, but can be hard to remember when carving. Have a look at the two examples below to see the difference between when you carve the linework of a motif versus when the motif is the relief (i.e. the lines have been carved around).

2. When drawing your design consider the use of positive and negative space. Positive space refers to the subject or areas of interest in an artwork, whereas negative space is the area that surrounds the subject. While it might be tempting to consider negative space as the section of a block that is carved, this is not necessarily always the case. In example 1 and 2, the negative and positive space is technically the same but in the first illustration the positive space is carved and in the second illustration the negative space is carved. Negative space can help to balance a print or focus the subject, so it is important to consider how we treat it. Do you want it to be solid (like in example 1) or do you want the background to be the colour of the paper (carved away like in example 2).

3. Remember that if you have a particular orientation for a design, or if your design includes text, you need to reverse the image on the block so that it prints the correct way. (Note: if you use the tracing paper transfer method on page 26, your design will be reversed automatically.)

4. Keep the design for your first block relatively simple. It is easy to get carried away and draw a very intricate design, but fine carving takes practise. When you are a beginner, it is difficult to get the same level of detail when wielding a carving tool as you get with a pencil. But by all means, prove me wrong!

EXAMPLE 1   EXAMPLE 2

1.

2.

3.

4.

5.

1. DRAWING A DESIGN

2. TRANSFERRING THE DESIGN ONTO RUBBER

3. CARVING THE STAMP

4. INKING THE STAMP

5. PRINTING

Transferring your design

While you can draw directly onto your rubber or lino, I prefer to perfect my design on paper and then transfer it using one of the following methods.

Tracing paper method

For easy-carve rubber (and for some kinds of lino), the best way to transfer a design is to use tracing paper (or baking paper at a pinch). I prefer this method because the tracing paper automatically reverses the design onto the block, so that when it is printed, it will be correct. This is particularly useful when you are printing text.

1. Trace your design with a pencil. A slightly heavier pencil like a 2B works best.
2. Check your carving material for indents or pockmarks (these will show in your final block, so it's best to avoid them if possible).
3. Flip your tracing paper over and place the pencil-marked side onto the carving material. If you have a large design that will take a little while to transfer, you might like to secure it to your carving material with a piece of tape.
4. Using something firm and blunt such as a bone folder, the end of a pencil or even your fingernail, rub all your lines. As you go, you can check to see how well the design is transferring and use more pressure if required.

It is possible to do this with copy paper – I simply prefer tracing paper because it is see-through, so if the paper shifts before I have finished transferring the design, I can simply move it back into position.

Carbon paper transfer method

If you would prefer to only draw your design once (and you don't particularly care about its orientation) you might choose to use carbon paper or graphite paper to transfer your design. This method works well on most lino and wood, but does not really work on rubber.

1. Place your carbon or graphite paper, carbon-side down, on your carving material. If you are concerned about it slipping, secure it in place with tape.
2. Put your design on top of the carbon paper. Secure this in place as well.
3. Use a pen or pencil to draw over the lines of your design, checking as you go and altering the pressure as necessary.

Preparing your block

At this stage, you may want to trim your block down to make it easier to manoeuvre while carving. If you are cutting down lino, try to trim down the hessian strands so that they don't become too raggedy. If you are concerned that you might lose your design (via smudging or rubbing), you could go over it with a permanent marker or a ballpoint pen. If you do this, be aware that sometimes the pen ink can transfer to your eventual print, depending on the colour of the block printing ink (especially yellow). It is sometimes a good idea when starting out to use two colours of pen – one for the lines you want to keep and another for the sections of the block that you want to carve. Just remember which is which!

Another tip is to stain your rubber, lino or wood prior to carving. Depending on the colour of your material and the intricacy of the carving, it can sometimes be difficult to see where you have already carved. You can counter this by staining lino or wood with Indian ink, or by pre-inking the rubber with a contrasting colour inkpad. For example, the easy-carve rubber that I use is bright white. When I carve under a light, the glare on the PVC rubber can make it challenging to see my carving lines. If I blot the rubber with a sepia inkpad and remove the excess with copy paper, I am left with a very light brown rubber. The carved white lines are then easy to differentiate from the uncarved brown rubber.

Carving your first stamp

Once you have successfully transferred your design to your carving material and prepared your block, it is time to get the tools out. Cutting tools are not pens, and should not be held like them either. Hold the tool in the palm of your hand with the bottom of the 'V' or 'U' on the surface of the rubber. Your index finger will rest on the top of the gouge and help to direct the tool and regulate the pressure you apply to it. When you want to carve, gently apply a little pressure to the tool so that it digs into the rubber, and push the tool away from you. Always carve away from your body and try to keep your fingers behind your cutting tools. Finish your cut by easing the pressure, thus resulting in a piece of rubber or lino coming away from the block.

Practise carving on a spare piece of rubber before starting your actual stamp so that you can experiment with pressure and depth. The pressure you apply affects the cut you make. The harder you push, the deeper the cut. Likewise, changing the angle of your cutter will change the cut. If you have multiple tools, play with all of them to learn how they are best used and what marks they can make.

Before you start to carve your design, have a plan as to what you are cutting away and what remains.

Let's use the flower design as an example again. In example 1, we carve the petals and the lines of the stem and the leaves. The background is solid and uncarved so will be printed. In example 2, we carve *around* the petals, the stem and the leaves, and carve the veins. A common mistake is to carve around the petals and leaves but to then carve away the stem line (which would be a problem). This is where it may be good to use different-coloured pens as a visual reminder of what *not* to cut! The background is carved, and the grey line represents where the stamp might be trimmed with a craft knife.

Go slowly but consistently. Try to carve long, even, continuous cuts. Remember that you can always cut more away, but once it's carved, you can't put it back! Even a slight scratch on the surface with your tool will show up in a print, so take it easy.

When carving curves, turn the piece of rubber rather than your hand and your tool. This is easier to do when you have a smaller block. Therefore, if you have a large piece of rubber and a small design, consider cutting your design out in order to make the stamp easier to move as you carve it.

If you are not sure whether you have carved deeply enough, ink up your block and test how it's printing. Depending on which cutter you use, you may find that you end up with little ridges when you carve out larger sections. These little ridges may not be as high as the relief but they might be high enough to get a little ink on them and show up on your print. This is called 'noise'. Sometimes, noise is welcomed – it can add movement or texture to a print – and other times it is not the look we are going for. Testing your block along the way by inking with an inkpad will help you decide whether you want the noise or not.

Finally, carving is a skill that takes a lot of practise to refine. Remember to take breaks, and roll your shoulders every now and again to avoid hunching or stress to your neck. Most importantly, take it easy on yourself and enjoy the process. Everything looks better hand-printed, so don't worry if you cannot achieve fine or precise lines in the beginning. Part of the charm of block printing is that the results look rustic and handmade, and this is one of the reasons you might stamp an image rather than draw it or produce it digitally.

EXAMPLE 1

EXAMPLE 2

Inking and printing

Once your block is carved, it is ready to ink up and print. The majority of the projects in this book are made with smaller blocks, which can be stamped (pressed down) onto a substrate. When stamping, inkpads are the easiest and cleanest option. By cleanest, I don't mean that there is no mess – ink in general is messy – but rather that stamping with an inkpad produces a crisp image, whereas acrylic paint or relief printing ink sometimes causes the stamp to slide when pressed on the paper, which can lead to a slightly squashed print.

While everyone knows how to use a stamp, I do have some tips for a successful print. Firstly, make sure you *always bring the inkpad down onto the block* rather than the other way around. This ensures that the whole block gets evenly covered. Secondly, when stamping, press the block down firmly and carefully onto your paper. Keep applying pressure *without moving the block* making sure that *the whole block* makes good contact with the paper.

Pulling a print

Blocks over 15 x 15 cm (6 x 6 in) can become unwieldy and difficult to print. Therefore when printing large blocks, I would suggest you switch to the method of laying the paper over the block and pulling a print. This way of printing is more in keeping with traditional lino printing and woodcut printing.

Neither inkpad ink or acrylic paint work well when pulling a print (inkpad ink benefits from being pressed down into the paper, while acrylic paint is so quick drying that it can often rip the paper when you try to pull the print). For these reasons, I always use relief printing ink when I want to pull a print. Relief printing ink is tacky, and so the paper is unlikely to move once it has been laid on the block. It also remains 'open' for longer and so the paper comes off the block with ease.

To ink up a block with block printing ink, begin by squeezing out a line of ink onto a print plate or tray. Use your brayer to roll out the ink – you are aiming for a nice even coverage on the brayer and across the plate. You will know when you have hit the sweet spot of just enough ink because you will hear it and see it: TSHIC! TSHIC! TSHIC! – it should sound a little like a car driving on a wet street, and the ink should look velvety (if you have little peaks, you have too much ink). Roll your inked brayer across the surface of the block and try to keep it smooth and consistent. Keep an eye out for any stray hairs or specks (or left-over bits of rubber) that may get rolled onto the block – these will show up as anomalies in your print. Take care to wipe your fingers as you go (relief ink stays wet and tacky for ages and can spread far and wide if you are not careful). I always keep a packet of cleaning wipes nearby.

Aside from block printing ink, my main concern when pulling a print is block placement. This is how I line up my paper to my block.

1. Cut a piece of cardboard to the size of the paper you plan to print. For example, if you plan to print an A4 size print, then the cardboard should be A4.
2. Place your block where you want it on the carboard. If you are doing multiple prints and you want it to be in the same place every time you might like to draw guidelines around the block.
3. Ink up your block and place it on the cardboard.
4. Choose one of the bottom corners of the cardboard. Beginning with that corner, carefully line up your paper with the cardboard and lay the paper down on top of your inked block.
5. Burnish the paper with either a spoon or a baren. Check how the transfer is going by carefully lifting the corner of your paper.
6. Pull your print off the block and put it somewhere safe to dry.

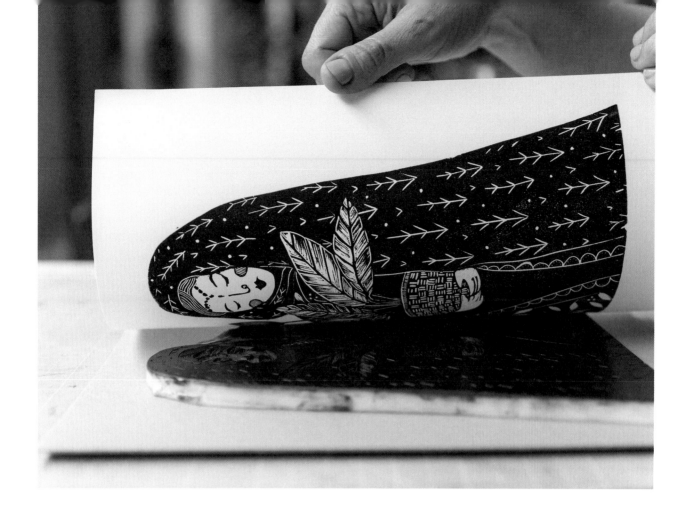

Cleaning up!

Try to stamp off as much ink as possible before cleaning your block. What you clean your blocks with depends on what kind of ink you use on them. Water-based inks should be cleaned with water. Oil-based inks can be removed with vegetable oil or linseed oil (although some pigments are more difficult to shift than others). Oil-based, water-washable relief inks are easy to wash up in hot water and a little washing-up liquid (dish soap). Use paper towels/rags or a soft toothbrush to clean your blocks, and be careful not to be overly vigorous with your cleaning so as not to break off any finer details.

Playing with colour and pattern

Once you have mastered basic stamp carving, you can start to play with colour and pattern. Aside from the simplest option of changing the colour of your ink, there are multiple ways in which you can use colour and pattern to enhance your block printing.

Spot colours

In some cases, you may want colour in specific sections of your print. In order to do this you can create spot colour blocks.

To create a spot colour block:
1. Print your main block (also known as the key block) on to copy paper.
2. Lay a piece of tracing paper on top and trace any sections of your motif that you would like to colour in.
3. Flip over the tracing paper and transfer the marking on to another piece of rubber.
4. Carve into a stamp, then ink up with desired colour and print on the corresponding space on the main motif.

Depending on the shape of the section you are trying to colour, sometimes spot colour blocks can look very odd.

Sometimes though, the blocks can work as a print by themselves. In this pictured example, I carved the key block, which I printed in green, pink and purple, and then carved the second block to colour in the negative space. However, as you can see in the smaller piece next to the main print, you can print a repeating pattern with the second stamp as well.

We play with spot colour in the Cosmetics Zip Pouch project on page 104.

Multi-colour blocks

Using inkpads

Another way that you can incorporate colour into your prints is by blending colour directly onto the block before printing it. This works particularly well with inkpads, particularly smaller cubes or teardrop inkpads. Put the lightest colour on first and then, using a bouncing/blending motion with your inkpad, apply your darker colours. Note that if you start with the darker colour and try to apply the lighter colour, you can damage your inkpad. For example, a deep brown inkpad can cope with a little orange, but a yellow inkpad will seldom recover from being contaminated by a darker colour. Depending on the design, you should also try to work from the middle out.

Using an ink gradient

Another option for incorporating more colour into a print is by using a gradient roll on your block. You can choose to make a gradient that uses tones of the same colour or one that combines multiple colours.

To prepare a gradient roll:

1. Get an appropriately sized brayer, like the one pictured – you need a brayer that will be wide enough to cover your whole block, or close to it.
2. On your printing plate, squeeze out some of each colour in your chosen gradient next to each other.
3. Take the brayer and roll out the ink. While rolling, try to develop a good mix between the colours without losing the original colours.
4. Try to roll the gradient onto the block with as few passes as possible. If you shift your brayer up or down as you roll, this will change the gradient. You are looking for a smooth transition between colours.

Overprinting or print layering

Overprinting or print layering refers to the technique of printing the same block multiple times on top of itself with different colours or shades of the same colour. The overlapping motifs and shapes can lead to happy accidents, such as interesting new colours, focal points or unexpected negative space. I use overprinting in the Foam-printed Reversible Planter Bag on page 110, but have a look at the following examples to get a sense of how layering prints in different ways can have different effects.

In the example to the right, the block is first printed with a light colour and then inked up again with a darker colour before being deliberately misregistered. The effect has a fun, 'out of focus' feel to it.

In the example below, the first layer of 'XO' was printed in rows of yellow and blue. The second layer was printed in red only. Here, the yellow and blue in the first layer provide pleasing contrast, whereas the use of red only in the second layer pulls the print together by providing continuity.

In the example above, the block is printed with two shades of green. The first layer was printed in light green and the block was rotated each time it was pressed to make the pattern feel less repeated, more random. The second layer was printed in dark green and the first time it was pressed, the block was shifted over and down. In this way, the second layer does not repeat the first layer but instead rhymes with it.

In the example on the left, the same block has been printed in three different colours – first yellow, then pink and then teal. As each layer was printed, the block's position was shifted so that by the end, there was very little negative space. While this is a bold print with its layering of contrasting colours, the overall effect is balanced because of the layered repetition of the motif.

Ghost printing

Ghost printing is the term used to describe the process of printing an already-printed stamp a second or even third time, without re-inking your block. When you print the stamp again you get a lighter or 'ghost' print. While there is a thrifty element to this technique – it's a great way of making your inkpad go further – I like to use ghost printing as a means to add tonal variation, dimension and depth to my printing. Note that if you print your block over the edge of your paper and then print the block again, you may end up with uneven ghost print.

In the example on the bottom left, I used ghost printing to get multiple tones that harmonise with one another. I particularly like the way in which the ghost prints interact with each other and with the solid prints to provide yet more tones.

For the middle example, I used ghost printing to give a sense of depth or dimension. While the leaves or branches in the foreground are solid and the subject of the focus, the ghost printing gives the impression that there are many more leaves in the background.

In the example on the bottom right, I used ghost-printed diamonds to provide a colourful subtle background to the solid printed pattern stamp. If I had used a solid printed diamond as the background, the pattern stamp would have got lost in the saturated colour.

Jigsaw printing

The final way that you can play with colouring your prints is by using a technique called jigsaw printing, which involves dividing your blocks into separate pieces. This enables you to create a seemingly complex multi-coloured print. The technique for creating a jigsaw print is similar to that for creating spot colour blocks.

1. Begin with your initial sketch and consider your colour choices.
2. Use your tracing paper to trace each of the separate shapes and carve them as separate blocks.
3. Now you get to the fun part of printing (and constructing) your jigsaw print. The simplest way of doing this is to begin with the biggest section and use that as a reference point for the rest of your print. In the case of the ramen print on page 40, I began with the blue bowl and then printed the noodles inside. That gave me a reference for the blocks that are left.

You can use the jigsaw method when you are pulling a print as well. To make the print on the right, I carved the whole block and then, using a scalpel, I carefully cut out the individual flowers. When it came to printing, I inked the green key block and then carefully inked up the pink flowers and inserted them back into the block in order to print the whole block at once. It can be challenging to put the cut-outs back in when they are inked. I try to remove a little more of the main block so that the cut-outs go back in more easily, and I push them down by pressing on a carved area, often using a blunt tool to assist. Of course, I could have approached this print another way by stamping the flowers separately after the green block was printed – same result, different process.

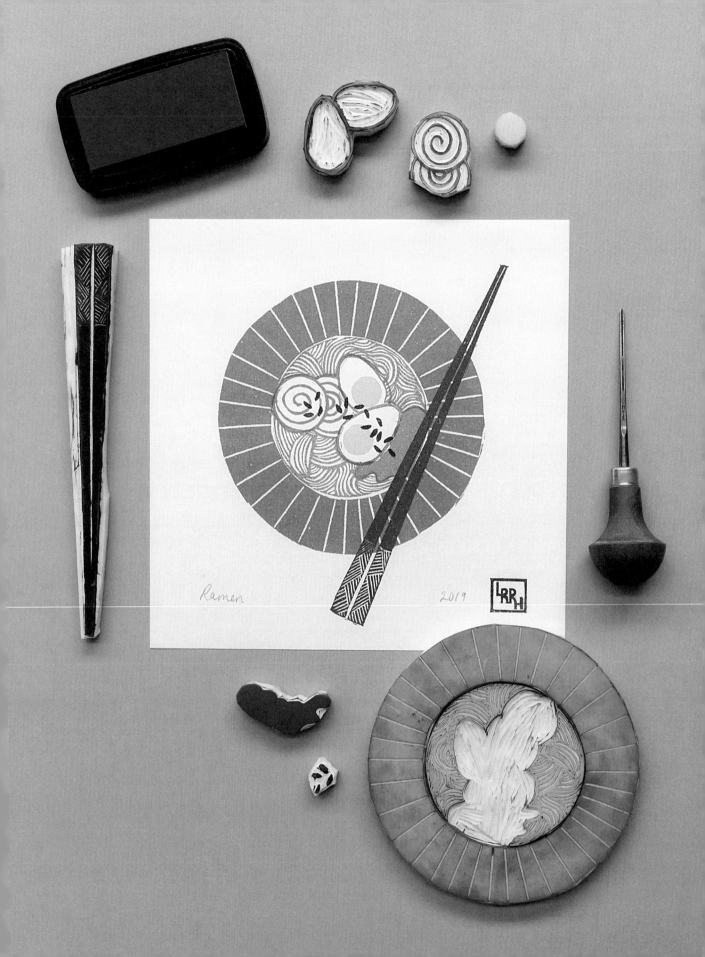

Ramen   2019   LRRH

Print registration

When it comes to making a repeat pattern or printing spot colours, one of the questions I get asked the most is: 'How do you manage to line up your blocks so perfectly?' The first thing I always say is that perfection is overrated, and that I prefer to live by the motto 'near enough is good enough' – and this is certainly how I approach block registration. I prefer it when blocks *don't* align perfectly – it adds to the hand-crafted feel of a piece. It must also be said that the more practise you have, the better you get. Nevertheless, let me give you a few tips.

Cut away excess rubber around your block. When you turn over your block, it is hard to know where your motif begins and ends. If you trim your stamps up to the edge of the relief, then it is far easier to print your block side by side or on top of one another.

Pick one or two key points to help you line up your block. It is possible to have too much information, and if you try to line up a print position by making sure all the sides are in the right place, you will inevitably end up disappointed. Pick just one or two key spots on your block to help you register it. (Even closing one eye will make it easier to print your block.) You can mark them with pencil on the back of the block to make it easier to remember. Likewise, if you are printing a spot colour, mark a spot to help you line it up with the key block.

There is no one way to register your blocks and you should use the tools that work for you. For example, I know many people who stick their rubber stamps to transparent acrylic blocks to help them line them up properly. (Acrylic blocks can also be particularly useful if you are working with thin rubber.) I sometimes use a pencil and ruler to make registration marks on the paper to help me place a block, and if I am creating a multi-block print and I need to lay the paper in exactly the same way, I will create a jig and use registration pins and tabs.

Masking

Sometimes you may want to protect a motif that has been printed or protect negative space (like a border around a print, for example). In this case, you can use a mask. The purpose of a mask is to protect the area underneath it; you can print up to and over the mask, but the paper underneath will remain unprinted.

A mask can be made out of paper, cardboard, stencil film or Frisket low-tack masking film. The thinner the mask, the crisper the line will be where the print and the mask meet.

We use masking in the Masked Greeting Card project on page 56 and in the Stamped Monogram Art project on page 70.

Patterns

One of my favourite aspects of block printing is the ease with which it allows me to make patterns. As humans we are drawn to patterns – they allow us to extract order from the chaos around us. It is not surprising, therefore, that printing a pattern is so innately satisfying. There are multiple projects in this book that require some form of patterning, so let's talk about what makes a pleasing pattern and some aspects to consider.

Repetition
All patterns have an element of repetition. The simplest pattern involves the repetition of a single motif (see below).

We can make a single motif pattern more fun by playing with placement and orientation. Look at the multiple ways that this simple flower tile stamp can be printed.

Contrast

Contrast is an important element in pattern-making. We can provide contrast by playing with colour or scale. For example, with the eye pattern on the opposite page (bottom right), the key motif is the same, but the colour of the iris changes. Similarly, in the Scandi flowers (top left), the interest comes from both the colour of the blooms and the orientation of the flowers. In the pomegranate pattern (bottom left), the contrast comes from the differing scale. While the whole and half pomegranates are of a similar size, the small scale of the pomegranate seed helps to provide contrast AND unify the pattern by repeating in and around the other shapes.

Group like with like

Another way to create an interesting pattern is by printing stamps that go together thematically. I love picking a theme like 'sweet treats' or 'creepy crawlies' and spending a little time drawing things relating to that theme. I like to choose at least three of those designs to create stamps. Those stamps could each create a simple pattern by themselves, but they are more effective when they are printed together.

Space matters

Let's talk about positive and negative space again. As we have already discussed, positive space refers to the subject or areas of interest, while negative space is the area surrounding the subject. The interplay between negative and positive space can really make itself be felt when we are creating patterns.

Look at these three pictures, for example. All three patterns have been made with the same stamp (albeit using different shades of blue), but by changing the placement, the amount of negative space changes. This, in turn, can change how the pattern resonates with someone. For me, the first pattern feels quite stark, and it almost seems like the white squares have a higher priority on the page. By getting rid of the negative space altogether in the third pattern, I find my eye is drawn to the sideways diamond shapes formed by the carved lines inside the cross. The second pattern feels the most balanced to me. How do these patterns make you feel? Are you drawn to one more than another?

Creating large pattern stamps (non-seamless)

When I am printing fabric, I deliberately make a larger block so that it takes less time to print a larger area. I also try to create a block that has a balance between positive and negative space.

1. Begin with a paper square measuring 10 x 10 cm (4 x 4 in) or 15 x 15 cm (6 x 6 in).
2. Pick a theme (I chose florals) and start to draw some simple motifs. Start with three main motifs and then start to fill the negative space with smaller motifs. Try to fill the space close to the edge so that you won't be left with too much negative space between the stamps.
3. When you have carved the stamp, mark one of the corners on the back of the stamp.
4. As you print the stamp, you have two options. You can print the stamp in the same orientation, keeping the corner mark in the same position each time. Or, do as I do and rotate the block, moving the corner mark around 90 degrees each time. This helps to provide rhythm and repetition in the pattern.

Tessellations

A tessellation is the repetition of shapes, with no overlaps and no gaps. Designing a stamp that seamlessly connects is like a gymnastic session for your brain. The easiest way to make a tessellated pattern is to use geometric shapes. The simplest and most obvious shape to use is a square, which can tessellate in a grid or a brick layout.

The example on the right is the simplest version of a repeating square tile stamp. Note that in this first example the motif is horizontally, vertically and diagonally symmetrical. There are also two repeating motifs – the central motif (A) and the corner motif (B), which does not fully reveal itself until all four corners are printed. (Note that, if this square was printed in a brick layout, only two of the corners would connect.)

As you might have already noticed, you could produce this pattern in another way, by simply carving one of the quarters and rotating it as you print it. This is called a quarter-tile stamp. In the example below, see how the two corner motifs have as much weight as the other. You can rotate the pattern around Corner A, but you can also rotate the pattern around Corner B.

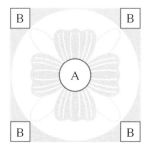

ROTATING QUARTER-TILE STAMP

ROTATING
QUARTER-TILE
STAMP

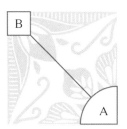

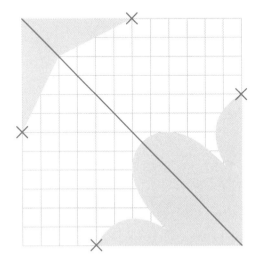

The best way to design these tiles is by using graph paper. The graph paper lines help to make sure that the motifs are symmetrical. This is particularly important at the edges of the stamp otherwise the stamp will not print seamlessly.

Other shapes that tessellate easily are equilateral triangles, diamonds and hexagons. These shapes work well together because they have a relationship: two equilateral triangles form a diamond and three diamonds or six equilateral triangles form a hexagon. Six diamonds and 12 equilateral triangles form a six-pointed star and so on. Knowing these gives you a lot of options in terms of playing with patterns.

Some geometric shapes, such as pentagons and octagons, do not connect seamlessly. However, the space between the shapes can create repeating stamps that become part of the overall pattern. Can you see the four-pointed stars in the above example of a repeating pentagon?

You can step outside regular geometric shapes and make tessellations using the following formula. In this example, I create a scallop (one of my favourite shapes) but you can use the same technique to create other mirrored tessellations.

1. Take a rectangular piece of paper. I like to use a piece that measures twice as long as it is high. Fold the paper in half.
2. Draw a curve (or a more intricate line if you want) and cut. You should now have two symmetrically cut pieces.
3. Move each piece to the bottom opposite edge of the unfolded original piece so the right-angled corners of the cut pieces meet up as shown.
4. Tape the pieces together. Now you have your tessellating shape. You can use the vertical middle line as a line of symmetry (a) or you could have fun and create little characters (b).

While I have demonstrated a mirrored tessellation (one that's the same on each side) you could create another kind of tessellation by leaving the paper unfolded and cutting a different line for each side. Taking it even further, if you take your cut pieces and, instead of moving them to the opposite side, move them vertically while rotating until the corners meet, you will have a rotational tessellation. In both of these cases, you will end up with a very strange shape, which you can then doodle a design. The only limit is your imagination.

1.

2.

3.

4.
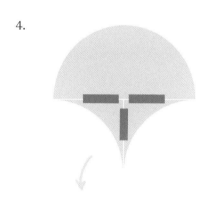

a

b

Projects

Masked greeting card

Celebrate your partner or best friend with this 60s-inspired greeting card. This project includes masking and ghost-printing, and you can also use this technique to make a birthday, Christmas or Valentine's card.

MATERIALS

plain cardstock or scored card
hand-carved sentiment stamp
    (see template on page 132)
inkpads (I've gone for 3 fairly
    retro psychedelic colours,
    but you do you!)
blank copy paper

scissors
hand-carved floral stamps
    (see template on page 133)
    for outer print

Masked greeting card

1. Find the middle of one half of your card and print your 'I got you babe' stamp (or whatever sentiment you choose). Let the ink dry.
2. Cut a shape out of copy paper. I chose a heart shape, but you could use a circle, an oval or a square.
3. Place your paper shape over your printed sentiment. This is your mask.
4. Start to use your floral stamps to print the background of your card. Try to print your motifs around the entire edge of the shape. Press firmly when you print over the edge of the mask in order to keep the edge of your printed shape crisp and clean. Play with printing your stamps twice for tonal variety and interest.

5. Carefully remove your mask and allow the ink to dry.
6. If using cardstock, score and then fold in half to make up your card. Write inside the finished card and pop it in an envelope.

TIPS

A border stamp helps to bring a little more focus to your sentiment.

TAKE IT
FURTHER

While you are printing a greeting
card, why not hand print a matching
envelope? To make an envelope to
fit an A6 card, use your floral stamps
to decorate a piece of copy paper
measuring 21 x 21 cm (8¼ x 8¼ in).
With the printed side facing down,
rotate the paper so that it looks
like a diamond and place your card
lengthways in the middle. Fold in the
two sides, of the paper and crease,
then unfold. Fold the top and bottom
flaps and then unfold. Cut the corner
triangles out with scissors. Stick the
sides to the bottom with a glue stick
or double-sided (double-stick) tape.

Upcycled card gift tags

Making your own gift tags to help decorate a present is like the icing on a cake – it's an extra detail that increases the 'wow' factor of your gift. And why buy gift tags when they are so easy to make? In this project, we recycle cardboard packaging into colourful gift tags.

MATERIALS

cardboard packaging raided
  from the recycling bin
scissors
sandpaper (optional)
gesso
paintbrushes
acrylic paint

hand-carved stamp
inkpad
pencil
ruler
hole punch
kitchen string, ribbon, butcher's
  twine, raffia, material offcuts

Upcycled card gift tags

1. Cut down your cardboard into manageable pieces to print. We will be decorating the printed side of the packaging and leaving the blank side available for a message to the receiver. If the cardboard is particularly glossy, lightly sanding it will allow for more effective paint coverage.

2. Apply a coat of gesso to the printed side of the cardboard. Allow to dry.

3. Paint over the dried gesso with acrylic paint. You can experiment here with different colours or even different painting tools. I like to use an old credit or key card to swipe paint over the cardboard which makes for interesting texture. Try to avoid thick layers of paint though, as these are harder to block print over. Allow to dry.

4. Ink up your stamp(s) and get printing. Try not to leave too much negative space between your motifs. Even better, try using a repeating pattern stamp. I used a repeating diamond stamp for my gift tags. Cover the entirety of your cardboard. Leave the ink to dry.

5. Flip over the cardboard and use your pencil and ruler to draw a grid so that you end up with tags that measure 9 x 5.5 cm (3½ x 2¼ in).

6. Cut out your tags and use your hole punch to make a hole in the top of each one.

7. Loop some string, raffia or material through each tag and personalise with a cute message.

TIPS

While scissors can suffice when making gift tags, there are many cute cutting devices on the market for making more intricately shaped gift tags – from one-design hand-held cutters to die-cutting machines to computerised machines.

For a super quick option, you can buy manilla shipping tags from office supply shops or an art store.

TAKE IT
FURTHER

What to do after the gifting is done? Don't throw those gift tags away! They can be used as bookmarks or popped into a scrapbook. I often reuse my gift tags as journal fodder, sticking them into a page to avoid the 'empty page' dilemma. In fact, many artists use shipping tags (available in different sizes) to experiment with various techniques and then use the tags in collage or as a focal point on a busy journal page.

Gift wrap – three favourite techniques

Every year, I make it a personal mission to see how many presents I can gift that are wrapped in hand-printed gift wrap. I particularly like to personalise the gift wrap for the person whom the gift is for – so much so that the gift doesn't always need a label because the wrap makes it obvious who the recipient is. My (poor) kids have learnt never to rip into a gift from mum, but instead to carefully peel off the tape and unwrap gently so that the hand-printed paper can either be recycled or reused for collage. I've used many techniques for printing gift wrap over the years, but here are my favourite three.

Upcycled grocery bags

Carefully pull apart a paper grocery bag, then unfold and cut off any handles. You will be left with quite a large, printing surface that makes a decent piece of gift wrap. You can print with it on your grocery bag with any kind of stamp and any kind of ink or paint. As with fabric printing, when printing gift wrap, a larger stamp allows you to cover more ground. If you have a single motif, you can play with how much negative space you leave around it. You can also print a soft foam stamp or gelatine stamp in the background and print over the top.

Furoshiki – fabric gift wrap

While there is extra effort involved, I really love to wrap small presents in hand-printed fabric. In Japan, the art of wrapping or transporting items with fabric is known as *furoshiki*. In general, you start with a square of fabric, and the size and the method of tying is dependent on the object being wrapped. I like to use plain (solid colour) cotton, either white or coloured, and always cut the edges using pinking shears so that they don't fray (or you could hem them with a sewing machine for an even neater look). Print the fabric using fabric block printing ink as explained on pages 16–17. This method of gift wrap is bright and crafty. It is also eco-friendly (tape-free/plastic-free), sustainable and reusable. For example, depending on its size the fabric wrap could be re-used as a headscarf, or a napkin or for wrapping another gift.

Colourful deli or tissue paper

While butcher's or brown paper is inexpensive and easy to print, sometimes you want to get a little brighter and a bit more special. That's when I try to get my hands on some deli paper or tissue paper. Squirt some bright acrylic paint on an old credit card or old library card and swipe it across the paper. Repeat with a couple of complementary colours. When dry, grab a handmade stamp and print on top. The ink will take a while to dry on the acrylic layer, so be patient before you use this pretty paper to wrap something precious.

Stick your name on it!

Kids love stickers – even more so when the stickers feature their name. I myself have an uncommon name. When I was younger, if I was in a gift shop or bookstore, I used to look for my name in the racks of name stickers or magnets. Alas, while there was always 'Sarah' or 'Amy' or 'Rachel', there was never anything featuring my name. I save my children this heartache by designing and printing their own name stamps and stickers.

MATERIALS

pencil
paper
tracing paper
rubber
carving tools
ink
matte A4 sticker paper
scissors

Stick your name on it!

1. When designing your name stamp, there are a couple of things to consider:
   a. Typography – if you are not a confident carver, bold block letters work best. A more confident carver might tackle some calligraphy, playing with cute curlicues and embellishments. If you have a favourite font, use a computer programme to play with the size and spacing of your name and then print out the one you like best.
   b. Negative versus positive space – you may choose to carve out the letters of your name, leaving the background as positive space. If so, think about the shape that will enclose your name and incorporate it into your design before you start carving. Likewise, if you are going to carve *around* your name and carve out the negative background, consider beforehand whether you might like a border around your name.
2. Once you're happy with your design, transfer it to the stamp by tracing the image onto tracing paper with a pencil, then flipping it over and rubbing the image onto the rubber. Your text will now be in reverse. Remember: transferring in this way is the best way of ensuring that your name can be read when it is printed.
3. Carve the stamp.
4. Print the name stamp on your piece of sticker paper. Play with different coloured inks until you have a whole page with your name all over it.
5. Cut out your stickers and use them in your journal, in your books, on your drink bottle ... everywhere!

TAKE IT
FURTHER

You could upscale your sticker production by scanning or photographing the design and opening it in Photoshop. Use the application to duplicate the image (and play with the colours while you are at it) until you have a full sheet of names. You can then print the names on either matte sticker paper or printable vinyl for waterproof stickers. Cut the stickers by hand or using an electronic cutting machine, if you have one. If you are really keen, you can even send your images away to a sticker-making company and get a whole roll of stickers.

Stamped monogram art

A hand-printed monogram is a sweet and thoughtful addition to a child's room or nursery. In this project, we practise masking with the use of a single letter stencil. While I use repeating stamps for a patterned monogram, you could also use a combo of ghost printing and overprinting for great effect.

MATERIALS

light cardstock or cartridge paper
   (for your stencil)
pencil
craft knife or scissors
smooth watercolour paper
   or Bristol paper (background
   for print – the size is up to you)

washi or masking (low-tack) tape
inkpads
hand-carved stamps (I used three
   hexagon stamps, but you could
   use a single repeating stamp)
frame

Stamped monogram art

1. The size of your letter depends on the size of your substrate. As I was using an A3 piece of watercolour paper, which is 42 x 29.7 cm (16½ x 11¾ in), I chose to make my letter about 28 x 25 cm(11 x 10 in). Measure your substrate and decide upon the size of your letter. Either draw or print out the letter. It is best to use a simple font, as you will be cutting it out by hand. Try to use a light cardstock. If the paper is too thin, it will curl and/or the ink will soak through – but, if it is too thick, you will find it hard to print over the edge cleanly. Try to leave plenty of card around the outside of the stencil.

2. Cut out your letter stencil. Secure your stencil to the substrate with washi or masking tape.

3. Ink up your stamp and begin printing your pattern. I found it easier to work out the middle of the letter and to begin there.

4. When printing the edges of the letter, apply extra pressure to the stamp in order to make sure it prints a clean, crisp line.

5. As you reach the bottom or top of your letter, make sure you don't print over the top or over the bottom of the stencil onto your clean paper. Protect your negative space with some scrap paper.

6. When the whole of the inside of your letter has been printed, carefully remove the washi tape. Let the print dry and pop it into the frame.

Be careful when using washi or masking tape. To prevent it tearing the paper beneath, it can help to reduce the tackiness of the tape by laying it first on your clothing or sticking it onto scrap paper.

Take this monogram technique and use it everywhere. If printing on fabric, you could make your stencil out of freezer paper and iron it on to the fabric. This is particularly useful when you want to include floating elements or islands (the inside of letters like A or R, for example). If you use freezer paper, however, try not to remove it until the fabric ink is dry. You don't have to stop at letters – you can use this technique with any silhouettes.

Print collage still life

From misprints to the papers you use to test your blocks or clean your stamps, developing your block-printing skills leads to lots of waste paper. However, one person's trash is the same person's treasure! I like to recycle these papers by using them in collage pieces. In this way, a misprint can be transformed from a mistake into a stepping stone to a new creation. The thought that I can create something with the waste prints in turn enables me to be braver with my printing.

MATERIALS

misprints/messy papers/test
  papers
scissors
sketch paper
pencil
background substrate (card, wood,
  canvas)

ephemera (old books, scrapbook
  paper)
hand-carved stamps
glue or double-sided (double-stick)
  tape

Print collage still life

1. Have a look through your collection of misprints/printed papers. Pull out colours and patterns that sing to you. In this example, I was drawn to yellow and blue tones.

2. Try to reimagine those papers/patterns in a different context. It might help to begin cutting out shapes to help this process. For example, the yellow papers made me think of lemons.

3. On a separate piece of paper, sketch a simple composition that you can use to guide your cutting. Here, I made a quick drawing of a bowl of lemons on a table top.

4. Choose a background substrate. You could use card, canvas, paper or even wood. I used a piece of coloured Mulberry paper.

5. Continue cutting out shapes according to your composition, and try to 'audition' pieces as you go. Feel free to change your mind and your composition as you work. Perhaps you might supplement your collage papers with a specific stamped motif. For example, in my collage you can see that I made the lemons and limes out of yellow and green patterned paper, but I also cut out a specific half-lemon print. Here are some other things to keep in mind as you work:
   a. contrasting colours
   b. pattern versus solid colour
   c. light and shade
   d. adding other ephemera, such as pages from old books

STEP 2

6. Once you are happy with the placement of your paper pieces, it's time to stick them to your background substrate. If you have a paper background, you might find it better to use double-sided (double-stick) tape instead of glue, which can cause lighter papers to warp. Card, canvas and wood, on the other hand, can handle either adhesive. Also, keep in mind that if your collage papers were originally printed with water-soluble ink, a wet adhesive will reactivate the ink.

7. Sit back and admire how you turned lemons into lemonade!

TIPS

Sometimes your sketch will inform your collage, and sometimes the misprints/papers that you use will inspire the composition. I often change my mind and experiment as I go along, playing with contrasting colours or textures.

Print collage can be addictive. Don't be surprised if you find yourself printing more papers just so you can make more print collages.

TAKE IT FURTHER

Ever thought about animating a short scene? Cut-paper collage lends itself very well to stop-motion animations.

Potato-printed tote bag

The humble potato has many uses – I love them mashed, roasted, baked and ... printed. There is no need for any fancy tools here: just potatoes, a couple of kitchen utensils and some ink. Given that potatoes are best suited to chunkier shapes rather than fine details, potato printing tends to work best with abstract or organic prints. This is block printing at its most rustic. I have gone for a Bauhaus-inspired design in this project, and I've used fabric printing ink because I am printing a calico (muslin) tote bag, but you could use acrylic paint on paper. This is a great project to do with young children as potato printing is naturally messy and organic – you can do the cutting and they can do the printing.

MATERIALS

potatoes or sweet potatoes
knife
selection of kitchen utensils
  (stainless steel straw, fork,
  skewer, cookie cutters)
iron

plain calico tote bag
cardboard (optional)
fabric block printing ink or screen
  printing ink
foam rollers or brayers
inking plate

Potato-printed tote bag

1. Gather some potatoes or sweet potatoes. Try to get a selection of sizes and shapes. There is no need to peel them.
2. Cut the potatoes in half and look at the shapes this reveals.
3. While it can be fun to print the potatoes just as they are, try making marks on them with your kitchen utensils. Here are some ideas:
    a. A stainless steel straw can be pushed in to make polka dots.
    b. A fork can be used to make crosshatches.
    c. Cookie cutters can create different shapes.
    d. A skewer or paring knife can be used to cut lines.
4. Iron your tote bag. Consider putting a piece of cardboard inside it to give you a sturdy and smooth surface to print on.
5. Prepare your ink by rolling it out onto your inking plate with foam rollers or a brayer.
6. Use the foam rollers or brayer to ink your potatoes. You could also use a paintbrush or simply tap the potato block into the ink. Try not to apply the ink too lightly, but bear in mind that too much ink will result in the potato block sliding and smudging when printed, or that excess ink might fill any textural marks you have made.
7. Print your shapes on to the tote bag. Play with your composition – try repeating shapes, changing the direction and overlapping them for interest.
8. Allow the tote bag to dry and cure or heat set the fabric with an iron. Please note that different fabric inks may have different setting instructions – always read the instructions on the back of the products.

TIPS

If you have left-over ink, grab some brown paper and print some wrapping paper. Fabric inks can be used on paper.

The potato blocks will not last – they will go soft and mouldy if left for too long, although you can refrigerate them to extend their usage. Otherwise, embrace their temporary nature and compost them after an afternoon of printing.

Party polka dots!

Decorating for a birthday party can be as simple as printing polka dots on some cardboard. Okay, okay, this project might involve a little bit more work than that, but not that much more, and the results speak for themselves – bright and festive bunting with matching cupcake toppers. You could even carry on the theme with the invites and the party bags. There is no need for any carving here – everything is printed with simple objects that you can find in your house. This is another great project that young kids can get involved in.

MATERIALS

household objects to print with
 (see overleaf for ideas)
coloured cardstock
acrylic paint
brayer
pencil

scissors
hole punch
ribbon or string
glue
toothpicks

Party polka dots!

1. Gather your household printing tools. The aim of the exercise is to look for objects that will make a circle or dot when printed. I found a pencil with a rubber on the end, a couple of corks and a small cardboard tube. You could use jar lids, toilet rolls, bottle tops or the inside of a small roll of washi tape. Try to get a collection of varied sizes and textures.

2. Choose some acrylic paint that contrasts with the colour of the cardstock. Roll out the acrylic paint with a brayer and start printing, using your household items as stamps. IMPORTANT: Acrylic paint does not contain drying retardants and has less 'open' time than block printing inks. This means that once you have rolled out your paint, you need to work fast before the paint dries.

3. After you have printed your cardstock and let it dry, draw a long triangle for the bunting flags and a five-pointed star for the cupcake toppers on a separate piece of cardstock. Cut out the shapes and then use these as a template to draw more triangles and stars on the non-printed side of your printed cardstock. Cut out the shapes.

4. To assemble the bunting, punch two holes in the top of each triangle. Cut your ribbon or string according to how long you would like your bunting to be and then thread your ribbon or string through the holes.

5. To assemble the cupcake toppers, cut out circles of a contrasting colour cardstock and stick your stars to the circles with glue. Glue or tape the toothpicks to the back of the toppers. They're now ready to be placed on cupcakes.

TAKE IT
FURTHER

In the interest of keeping this
project very simple, I didn't include
any carved stamps, but you could
go all out and carve some number
stamps to print on the cupcake
toppers, bunting or carve letters
to spell out the name of the
birthday child on the bunting.

Paper lantern

Paper lanterns instantly provide ambience to a room, and never more so than when you have made the lanterns yourself. You could get very festive indeed by printing motifs for any celebration you may choose, such as Chinese New Year, Hanukkah, Diwali, Ramadan or Christmas. Regardless of the occasion, the key to this lantern is the type of paper you choose to print on. The best papers are thin, strong and translucent, like *kitakata*, or banana paper. You could also print on tissue or deli paper.

MATERIALS

hand-carved stamp using
   the template on pages 133–134
inkpad or relief printing ink
4 pieces of thin/translucent paper
heavy cardstock

craft knife
ruler
glue stick or craft glue
LED candle

Paper lantern

1. Ink up your flower stamp and use it to repeatedly print on the pieces of translucent paper in whatever pattern you like. Let them dry.
2. Trace the templates for the lantern sides and transfer to your heavy cardstock. Carefully cut out your lantern pieces with a craft knife and ruler. Make sure you cut the side slots widely enough to allow for the width of your heavy cardstock.
3. Glue the printed papers to the outside of the lantern pieces and let dry.
4. Construct the lantern by slotting the two pieces with the side tabs into the two pieces with the side openings. This can be tricky – take your time.
5. Place an LED candle inside and enjoy the ambience created by the warm glow of your beautiful lantern!

Hand-stamped drink coasters

If you have any kind of wooden furniture in your house, then chances are you need drink coasters. I have plenty of sets, and my children have been known to fight over their favourites when setting the table. Hand-printed drink coasters are an easy way to help theme a setting or just bring an extra bit of fun and colour to the table.

MATERIALS

wooden coasters (I bought my coasters from a local company that offers laser-cut wood shapes)
sandpaper
black gesso

masking tape (optional)
paintbrush
stamps (use the template on page 132 or design your own)
inkpad or relief printing ink
sealant, such as Mod Podge

Hand-stamped drink coasters

1. Check your coasters for any ridges or bumps and give them a gentle sand. A smoother surface will print better.
2. Paint the coasters with black gesso. If you are concerned about getting black on the edges of the coasters, you could protect them with masking (low-tack) tape.
3. For my coasters, I chose to make a stamp that would cover the whole coaster, but you could use whatever you like – including smaller motifs or a stamp that could be repeated across the coaster.
4. Print the coasters and set aside to dry.
5. Seal your coasters using the sealant and leave to dry before using.

Try printing on the coasters without painting them first. Archival pigment inks stamp nicely onto plain wood or MDF with very little bleed. However, unlike when printing on paper, it takes a *very* long time for the ink to dry. A good suggestion is to blot the coasters with paper to remove any excess ink.

The sealant is quite important in order for the coasters to become functional and not be damaged by spills or condensation.

TAKE IT FURTHER

For a glamorous look, try gold on black.

Why don't you try printing a puzzle? In the example on the right I printed on nine coasters with moth stamps using black pigment ink. I had intended the puzzle to be a gift for a toddler, but my 12-year-old and her friend found it surprisingly difficult!

Air-dry clay Christmas ornaments

Every year on 1st December, my family puts up the Christmas tree. With great pleasure, we unpack the Christmas ornaments, which we greet like old friends. With the exception of several random baubles, all of our ornaments were either bought overseas, gifted by friends or family or made with love. I like to give my daughters a new ornament every year. My hope is that these ornaments will be the foundation pieces for their own collections that they will cherish and add to. For this project, we will print on to air-dry clay. Playing with clay takes me back to my childhood; there is something so satisfying about rolling clay into balls, smooshing and kneading it before flattening it with a rolling pin. While real clay is messy and requires a kiln to fire, you can get a similarly satisfying experience and a 'ceramic' look using air-dry clay. These ornaments are another family-friendly project to do in the lead up to Christmas.

MATERIALS

air-dry clay (I prefer Staedtler Fimo Air Basic Modelling clay)
rolling pin
craft mat or clean kitchen board
cookie cutters, butter knife or clay modelling tools
hand-carved stamps
lino printing ink (optional – see tip on page 97)
skewer
sandpaper
sealant, such as Mod Podge (optional)
string for hanging your ornament (hemp cord, butcher's twine, kitchen string, raffia, embroidery thread)

Air-dry clay
Christmas ornaments

1. Break off a hand-sized wedge of clay. Start to manipulate and knead it until it's malleable. Add a little water to your fingers if the clay starts to dry out.

2. Use a rolling pin to roll out the clay on a craft mat or chopping board. Try to keep the thickness consistent as you roll. You need the clay to be smooth, so wet the surface to smooth over any cracks or crevices.

3. Once your clay is rolled out, you can cut out your shape with a cookie cutter, or free form with a bread knife or with clay modelling tools. Remove any excess clay (this can be used to make more shapes later).

4. For printing your shapes, you have two options:
   a. For an embossed look, simply press the stamp gently into the clay *without any ink*.
   b. For a coloured ornament, ink up the stamp with your colour of choice and gently press into the clay.

5. Poke a hole in the top of each ornament with a skewer.

6. Leave your ornaments to dry. Drying time will be dependent on where you live and the climate. The air-dry clay will turn from beige to white as it dries. Turn your ornaments over to make sure the underside is dry as well.

7. Once the ornaments are fully dry and hardened take them outside and smooth the edges with sandpaper. The back of the ornament can also be sanded, but avoid sanding the front.

8. If you like, you can protect your ornaments by sealing them. The sealant gives the ornaments the look of glazed ceramic. Unsealed ornaments look a little more rustic.

9. String up your ornaments and hang on your tree.

TAKE IT FURTHER

What ink to use? In my own experiments, I found that lino printing inks work best. However, if you only have inkpads, I have found that water-based pigment inkpads (such as VersaColor) get the best result.

There are multiple air-dry clays on the market – I have found that some are much smellier than others. A packet of clay goes a long way and will go even further if you make sure the clay does not dry out by sealing the opened packet between usages.

Simple shape cutters work best for the longevity of the ornaments (sticky-outy bits are in risk of breaking off when dry).

Don't sand the ornaments inside! The fine dust from the clay will get *everywhere*.

Make sure you use a low-tack sealant on your ornaments if you don't want them to feel sticky.

You can make other cute gifts by block printing on clay, like a small trinket bowl. First print a large piece of clay. Use a bowl as a mould. Cut out the clay. Lay the clay over the bowl and gently push into the bowl, taking care not to smudge the inked design. Let dry and remove the clay when it is half-dry.

Hand-printed beeswax wraps

Does anything smell better than beeswax? Beeswax wraps used only to be seen in farmer's markets and school fairs. These days, however, they have become mainstream as we all try to limit our use of soft plastics like cling film (plastic wrap). Having antibacterial properties, which make them perfect to use in the kitchen, beeswax wraps can cover bowls or jars, be made into sandwich bags, or be moulded around half-cut fruit, vegetables or even cheese. They are reusable, make fun gifts and are easy and inexpensive to make yourself.

MATERIALS

cotton fabric, washed
iron
fabric scissors
pinking shears (optional)
hand-carved stamps (or found objects)
fabric block printing ink or screen printing ink
old oven tray
oven
parchment paper/baking paper
beeswax (pellets or block)
grater (if using beeswax block)

Hand-printed beeswax wraps

1. Prepare your fabric for printing by ironing it and then cutting it to size. This is quite a good project for using up smaller scraps of fabric because you only need a small wrap (perhaps 15 x 15 cm/6 x 6 in) for covering jars. Or you could print a larger piece (50 x 50 cm/20 x 20 in) and then cut to the sizes you want. You might like to cut a variety of sizes and shapes depending on the containers you have in your kitchen. If you don't want the fabric to fray, use pinking shears to cut a zigzag edge around your wraps – the wax should stop the wraps from fraying anyway, but a zigzag edge does look pretty.

2. Print your wraps with your handmade blocks or found objects. It might be fun to use stamps that have a food theme or include bees. Given their smaller size, beeswax wraps are a good way to experiment with patterns or different colourways.

3. Let your fabric dry, heat set if required and launder.

4. Preheat your oven to 180ºC (350ºF) and prepare an old oven tray (wax is very difficult to remove so don't use your best one). Line your oven tray with baking paper, then lay your printed fabric over the baking paper.

5. If your beeswax comes in block form, grate the wax with a box grater and sprinkle over the fabric. If the beeswax comes as pellets, sprinkle these evenly over the fabric. If your fabric is bigger than the tray, fold it up and then add extra wax on the top of the fabric. The wax when melted should soak through all the layers.

6. Put the tray in the oven and watch like a hawk! A couple of minutes is all it takes for the wax to melt and soak through the fabric.

7. Remove the tray from the oven. Carefully lift the hot, waxed fabric from the baking paper and waft it gently for 10 seconds. The wax will dry quickly and the fabric will stiffen (plus your kitchen will smell AMAZING). Remove the baking paper from the tray.

8. Once dry, your wrap is ready to use, and you can feel very satisfied about doing a little good deed for the planet.

TIPS

This recipe is for a non-tacky beeswax wrap, which is good for covering and wrapping. If you want a tacky wrap (like the more commercial wraps and more like cling film/plastic wrap), you might want to use another method that uses pine resin (for tackiness) and jojoba oil (for fabric pliability). Crush 30 g (1 oz) of pine resin and add to 15 g (½ oz) of jojoba oil and 60 g (2 oz) of beeswax. Melt together in a bain-marie (it will take at least 30 minutes for the ingredients to mix). Using a cheap paintbrush that you don't mind sacrificing, paint the wax mixture on to the fabric until you have even coverage and then pop into the oven for a minute or two. Dry wraps and use. Any left-over wax mixture can be poured into an ice cube tray to be used another time.

Note the oil can cause your fabric ink to leach a little bit. I have found this seems to affect reds and yellows more than blues, greens and blacks.

Beeswax wraps can be cleaned with warm, soapy water. Do not use hot water and do not place beeswax wraps in the microwave – the wax will melt. Avoid wrapping liquids or meat with beeswax wraps.

DON'T THROW OUT OLD WRAPS!
Tatty, cracked wraps can be refreshed. A quick blast in the oven can help the wax to melt and reseal the wrap. If the wax has really deteriorated, then you can rewax.

Spot colour cosmetics zip pouch

In this project, we are going to use a lipstick motif to print fabric, which we will then turn into a simple zipper bag. A zipper pouch always comes in handy, whether it is used for holding makeup, odds, bits and bobs or pens and art supplies (maybe that's just me). A second stamp is used to add spots of colour to our pattern and make it pop! We will use a sewing machine in this project – it makes for a good basic project for those learning how to use a machine – but you could sew it by hand if you prefer. If neither of those options float your boat, you could print a premade zipper bag (see my note under Quick Fix at the end of the project).

MATERIALS

lipstick template on page 132
pencil
tracing paper
easy carve rubber
carving tools
2 pieces of plain (solid colour) cotton fabric, each at least 25 x 18 cm (10 x 7 in)
2 pieces of contrasting cotton lining, each at least 25 x 18 cm (10 x 7 in)

fabric block printing ink or screen printing ink (if the zipper pouch won't be washed you could use inkpads, relief printing ink or acrylic paint)
iron
pins
25 cm (10 in) zipper
sewing machine or sewing needle and thread

Spot colour cosmetics zip pouch

1. Trace the lipstick design on page 132 or draw your own. Transfer the design on to your rubber and carve your stamp. Trace the section of the design that you want to colour, then transfer it on to your rubber and carve a second stamp (see page 32 for more information).

2. Print your main motif on the fabric with fabric block printing ink or screen printing ink. I chose to print my main motif in black.

3. Print your second stamp with a contrasting colour. I chose to use red.

4. Let your fabric dry and cure or heat set it depending on which medium you use.

5. Time to sew your pouch. Pin your zip along one long side of your printed fabric as shown, with the front of the zip and the printed side of the fabric facing the same way (right side to right side) and with the edges aligned.

6. Match the other side of the zipper to the edge of the other piece of printed fabric (right side to right side) and stitch this side.

7. To attach the lining, sandwich the zipper between one piece of the lining and the printed fabric that it is already sewn to. You can stitch on the same stitching line as the first.

STEP 3

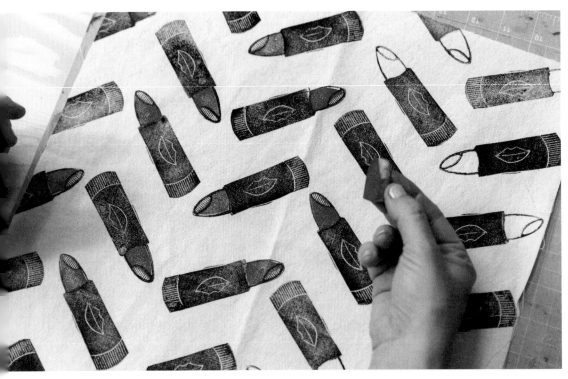

STEP 5

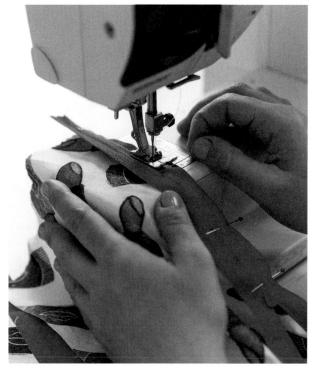

Spot colour cosmetics zip pouch

8. Repeat with the other side of lining.
9. Press your pieces and then topstitch alongside the zipper on the outer pieces.
10. Unzip your zipper three-quarters of the way (important for when you eventually turn the pouch out the right way), then lay out your pouch so that the lining pieces are right sides together and the printed pieces are right sides together. Make sure that all the seams including the zipper ends are facing towards the lining side. Pin together.
11. Sew a continuous seam of 1.5 cm (⅝ in) all the way around the pouch. Make sure that you leave a gap of at least 8 cm (3 in) on the bottom edge of the lining. This gap is for pulling your pouch through afterwards.
12. Snip across the corners of your pouch and trim back the edges of your lining.
13. Turn out your pouch by reaching through the unsewn gap and pulling the outer fabric through. Use the end of a paintbrush or a pencil to poke out the corners.
14. Sew the gap in the lining by turning under the fabric and topstitching close to the edge, or try hand stitching if you prefer.
15. Press and admire your handiwork.

STEP 7

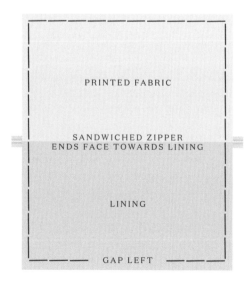

PRINTED FABRIC

SANDWICHED ZIPPER
ENDS FACE TOWARDS LINING

LINING

GAP LEFT

STEP 11

TIPS

Zipper bags can be as big or as small as you like. Simply cut your fabric to match the length of your zipper (or cut your zipper to match the length of your fabric).

Quick fix

If sewing is not your thing or you are short on time, look out for simple zipper pouches that could do with extra embellishment. When printing something pre-made, try to give yourself the smoothest printing surface possible by placing cardboard inside the zipper bag. A single motif might work best in this case, rather than a repeat pattern. Try to avoid printing over seams, as this will affect your print.

Foam-printed reversible planter bag

Indoor plants are such a great way of adding some green to your scene. While I love ceramic planters, it is just as fun to print and make my own containers. In this project, we are going to make and use foam stamps, and we will also use the technique of overprinting. This is another great project to do with kids, as it doesn't require carving.

MATERIALS

1 metre (1⅛ yards) of plain (solid colour) cotton or canvas fabric to print
1 metre (1⅛ yards) of cotton or canvas fabric in a contrasting colour
measuring tape
plastic plant pot and drip tray
pencil or fabric marking pen

foam stamps (page 21)
fabric block printing ink or acrylic paint in two contrasting colours
iron-on interfacing (optional)
iron (optional)
pins
rotary cutter and cutting mat or fabric scissors
sewing machine

Foam-printed reversible planter bag

1. Take your clean plant pot drip tray and turn it upside down on one end of your plain (for printing) fabric. Using your pencil or fabric pen, draw around the pot. Now use your measuring tape to add 1.5 cm (⅝ in) all the way around the circle. This is the base of your planter bag. To calculate the width your fabric needs to be, measure the diameter of the drip tray, then multiply it by 3.14 (Pi) and add 3 cm (1.25 in). So, for example, if the diameter of my drip tray is 21 cm (8¼ in), I will need to cut 69 cm (27 in) of fabric (21 x 3.14 + 3). To calculate the height your fabric will need to be, measure the height of your plastic pot and then add the amount that you would like the fabric to hang over. Cut both the base circle and the measured rectangle out of the plain fabric, and then cut indentical pieces out of the contrasting fabric.
2. Ink or paint your foam stamp with your first colour and print your fabric.

STEP 1

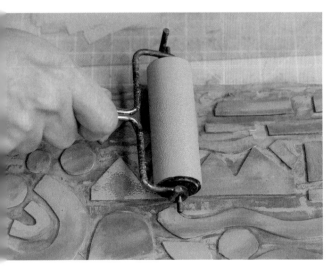

STEP 2

3. Ink or paint your foam stamp with your second colour and print your fabric. Pay attention to the placement of your stamp this second time. Try not to place the stamp in the same position – shift it over or turn it around. The interest comes from the overlapping shapes and colours.
4. Let your fabric dry/cure.
5. At this stage, if you are using a light cotton fabric, you may want to use interfacing or stabiliser to give it more structure. I used iron-on interfacing on the inside of my printed fabric.
6. To assemble the bag, fold your printed fabric in half, right sides facing, and pin the side edges together. Stitch together with a 3 cm (1.25 in) seam allowance to make a tube. Then pin the tube to the circle piece along the bottom edge with right sides together and sew with a 1.5 cm (⅝ in) seam allowance.
7. Clip notches in the seam allowance (this is to help to reduce bulk at the end).
8. Repeat steps 6 and 7 with the contrasting fabric pieces for the lining.

Foam-printed reversible planter bag

STEP 6

9. Now you have two simple bags. Turn one bag the right side out, then put the other bag inside it. Sew around the top of the bag using a 1.5 cm (⅝ in) seam allowance, but leave a 15 cm (6 in) gap between the beginning and the end of your stitching. Use this gap to turn the bag and the lining out the right way.

10. Topstitch 2 mm (⅛ in) all the way around the top.

11. Fold the planter over so the contrasting material is visible.

12. Your planter bag is ready to use. Make sure you pop the drip tray at the bottom of the bag before you put your plant pot inside.

STEP 9

Drum lampshade

Put your stamp on a living space with a hand-printed lampshade. The lampshade can be for a bedside lamp, a standing lamp or even a hanging pendant lamp.

MATERIALS

2 lampshade rings (1 fitted ring + 1 plain ring)
plain (solid colour) cotton fabric (see step 1 for fabric size requirements)
adhesive styrene sheet
measuring tape or ruler
hand-carved stamp (I recommend a larger block for printing a larger length of fabric)

fabric block printing ink or screen printing ink
iron
rotary cutter or fabric shears
craft glue or hot glue gun
bulldog clips
moulding tool or peg

Drum lampshade

1. Measure your fabric and your styrene. You want your styrene to measure the circumference of the lampshade rings plus 2.5 cm (1 in) for overlap. To get this measurement, use the following equation: lampshade diameter x Pi (3.14) + 2.5. My lampshade ring is 30 cm (12 in) in diameter, so I cut a length of styrene measuring 97 cm (38 in). For the fabric length, I add another 2 cm (¾ in) – so mine was 99 cm (39 in). The width of your fabric will be determined by the width of your styrene. My styrene was 23 cm (9 in) wide, and I wanted a good amount of clearance on both sides, so I cut my fabric to a width of 30 cm (12 in).

2. Ink up your stamp and print your fabric and let cure, or heat set it according to instructions.

3. Iron your fabric so it is as smooth as possible.

4. Lay your fabric out on a clean surface, printed side down. Peel back a little bit of the paper layer on the styrene to reveal the adhesive side and line up so one of the short edges of the styrene is flush with one of the short edges of the fabric, with an equal amount of fabric above and below the styrene's long edges. Slowly pulling back the paper layer, press down on the styrene so that it sticks to your fabric. Pull your fabric while doing this to get the adhesion as smooth as possible.

5. At this point, trim the fabric so that there is only 1.5 cm (⅝ in) excess along the top and bottom edge of the styrene and 1.5 cm (⅝ in) excess at the other short edge of the styrene.

6. At the short edge of the styrene where there is excess fabric, fold the fabric over the end of the styrene and secure it with glue.

While this project calls for a lot of specific materials, you could simply cover a plain white lampshade. Some homeware stores even sell lampshades that come flatpacked with plain white fabric that can be clipped and velcroed to the metal rings. These are perfect for block printing.

Drum lampshade

7. Roll your styrene into a cylinder and use the bulldog clips to hold it in place. Leave the arms of the top bulldog clip facing up. Then take the top lampshade rings and place it into the cylinder. Rest the ring between the arms of the bulldog clip you put down first, then use the other bulldog clips to secure the ring to the edge of the styrene. Do the same with the other lampshade ring. Make sure the edge of the styrene are lined up with the outer edge of the rings and adjust your cylinder as required for a snug fit.

8. Now it is time to glue. Working a few centimetres/inches at a time, apply glue to the inside edge of the ring and to the overhanging fabric.

Try to wrap the fabric around the ring, using a moulding tool or peg to help push the fabric in and around. Go slowly and gently and try not to get glue everywhere (especially on the styrene).

9. Glue down the folded edge of the lining over the flush edge for a neat finish.

10. Once the top ring is done, repeat with the bottom ring.

11. Once both rings are glued, carefully glue inside the side seam. Peg at the top and bottom and allow to dry for an hour.

12. Remove the pegs and voilà: your lampshade is ready to use.

STEP 4

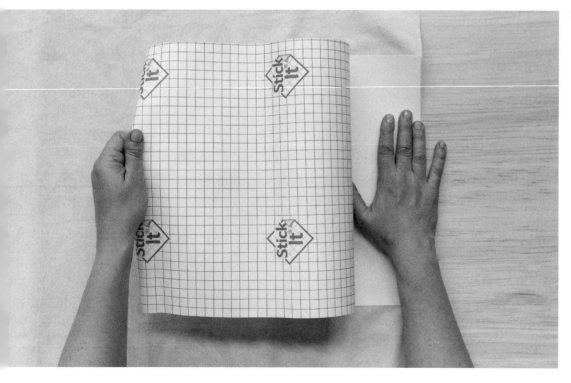

Just-like-leather wallet

By now, you will have seen that there are many materials you can block print on, including paper, fabric and wood. While you can print on leather, it is a complicated business involving hammers and metal stamps. Instead, this cute wallet is made out of Kraft-tex®, which is a paper-based leather alternative. It is easy to print, fun to sew and could be a nice gift for your vegan friends, as well.

MATERIALS

Kraft-tex®
ruler
pencil
rotary cutter and cutting mat
  or scissors
hand-carved stamps (try some fun
  repeating geometric stamps
  with bold lines and shapes)

inkpads (I used VersaFine Clair
  Chianti to get a deep rich brown
  on the tan Kraft-tex)
bulldog clips
sewing machine
iron

Just-like-leather wallet

1. Measure and cut your pieces of Kraft-tex. You will need two pieces measuring 23 x 9 cm (9 x 3½ in) for the wallet and two pieces measuring 22 x 5 cm (8¾ x 2 in) for the pockets.

2. Take the two larger pieces of Kraft-tex. One of these pieces will be the outside of the wallet and the other piece will be sewn with the smaller pieces to make the card pockets. When sewn together, these two pieces will also make a large pocket for cash. Ink up your stamp and block print these pieces accordingly. For example, I printed the outside piece of the wallet, but also printed the inner sides of the large pocket. I only printed the sections of the card pockets that would be seen. Once you're happy with your design, let your pieces dry.

3. Place the first pocket piece on top of the large inner wallet piece. The pocket piece is thinner and shorter than the large piece, and you need to position it so that you can see 1.5 cm (⅝ in) of the larger piece above, 5 mm (¼ in) on either side and 2.5 cm (1 in) below. Secure with bulldog clips. Using straight stitch, sew the lower edge of the pocket piece to the inner wallet 3 mm (⅛ in) in from the edge.

4. Carefully place the second pocket piece on top of the first two pieces. Line this piece up so that you can see 5 mm (¼ in) of the larger piece at the sides and 5 mm (¼ in) underneath. Secure all three layers with bulldog clips.

5. Fold all three layers in half and lightly mark the crease. Using straight stitch, sew 3 mm (⅛ in) on either side of the crease from the top of the first pocket to the bottom of the second pocket.

6. Using straight stitch again, sew around the three sides 3 mm (⅛ in) inside the pocket edges.

7. Line up the outer piece of the wallet with the inner piece of the wallet, with the cash pocket sides facing each other. Secure with bulldog clips.

8. Sew the bottom and two short edges together using zigzag stitch. Make sure you sew close to but not over the edge of the pieces.

9. Snip off any long threads. Fold the wallet in half and give it a good press with the iron and then it's ready to go.

STEP 6

TIPS

Because Kraft-tex is a paper product, you should use dedicated paper scissors or rotary cutters – don't use your best fabric shears – and a dedicated sewing machine needle. Use bulldog clips to secure your pieces of Kraft-tex together. Pins will leave holes. When beginning to machine sew the Kraft-tex try not to go back and forward more than once otherwise the Kraft-tex may perforate.

STEP 8

Print and stitch cushion

I am a hobby hoarder. By this, I do not mean that I like to hoard art supplies (although I do) but rather that I hoard hobbies. I love discovering and diving into new mediums or crafts. I read all the books and invest in the tools and get obsessed for several months. Sometimes these hobbies stick around for a while and sometimes they fall by the wayside, but I often bring something from them to apply to my printmaking. One craft that I have dipped into multiple times is embroidery – hand printing and stitching go so well together. The block printing gives textiles a wonderful hand-crafted feel, and needlework can add a textural or tactile element to a block-printed piece. Please note that we are not pushing the boat out with this project; the embroidery is only a simple running stitch. If you are comfortable with embroidery and know multiple stitches, feel free to play and embellish your pillow as you wish.

MATERIALS

- 0.5 metre (½ yard) plain (solid colour) cotton fabric for printing
- 0.5 metre (½ yard) contrasting fabric for back of pillow
- measuring tape
- rotary cutter and mat or fabric scissors
- cushion insert
- foam or hand-carved stamps
- fabric block printing ink
- iron-on interfacing (optional)
- iron (optional)
- embroidery hoop
- embroidery thread or floss
- embroidery needle
- zipper (the length will depend on the width of your cushion)
- pins
- sewing machine

Print and stitch cushion

1. Measure and cut the fabric for your cushion pieces. The amount of fabric you need will depend on the size of your cushion insert. To get the width of fabric required, take your measuring tape and measure loosely from one side seam of the cushion insert to the other side seam, then add 3 cm (1¼ in). This is the width for your fabric. Do the same for the height. Cut a piece of plain fabric for the front of the cushion cover and a piece of contrasting fabric for the back.

2. Ink up your stamp and print your plain cotton fabric. Let it dry and cure.

3. Place your embroidery hoop over a printed motif, then thread a needle with some contrasting embroidery thread and knot the end.

4. Use running stitch to embellish and add texture to your hand printing. Try stitching inside some motifs, and try adding stitched lines running across the negative space, perhaps linking motifs.

Experiment with how the stitching can accentuate your motifs.

5. There are no right answers as far as the stitching is concerned. Perhaps you may only want to stitch one small area as a point of interest, or perhaps you wish to keep working across the front of your pillow, adding stitches until you are satisfied. (Note: it is possible to embroider the cushion after it has been sewn, but it's easier to do so before.)

6. Once you are happy with your stitching, it is time to sew up your cushion cover. Lay out both the front (printed) cushion piece and the back contrasting colour piece. Find the bottom edge of each of the pieces, then fold over 1.5 cm (⅝ in) to the inside and press so that you have a nice crease.

7. Still working on the same edge of both pieces, unfold the edge and measure 5 cm (2 in) from either side. Mark with a pin.

STEP 2

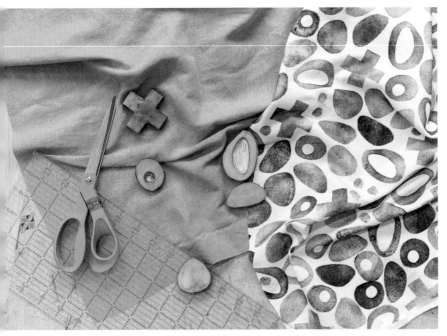

Print and stitch cushion

8. Take the two cushion cover pieces and lay them on top of each other with the right sides facing together. Line up the bottom edges and secure along the creased line. Sew along the creased line from the outer edge to the pin, taking care to backstitch at the pin. Repeat on the other side of the bottom edge.

9. If you lay out your cushion cover front and back with the right sides facing down, you should now see a gap for the zipper (see diagram below).

10. Measure 3 cm (1¼ in) from the bottom and the top of the cushion and mark with pins. Lay your zipper right side down, on top of the cushion cover opening. Pin the zipper head at the top 3 cm (1¼ in) mark and pin the bottom of the zipper at the bottom 3 cm (1¼ in) mark. (If your zipper is longer than necessary, don't worry! Pin in place and cut off the excess zipper.)

11. Starting at the top of the zipper, sew across the zipper, making sure to stitch back and forth to secure it. Sew down the first side of the zipper. When you get to the bottom of the zipper, stitch across several times to secure it, then sew up the other side of the zipper (see illustration for instruction).

12. IMPORTANT! Make sure that you leave your zipper open (or you will not be able to turn your cushion the right way after you have finished sewing it).

13. Pin the other three sides of the cushion pieces together (right sides together) and sew together using a 1.5 cm (⅝ in) seam.

14. Clip the corners and turn the cushion through the zipper opening.

15. Put your cushion insert inside your cushion cover and pop your creation in a cosy corner.

STEP 10

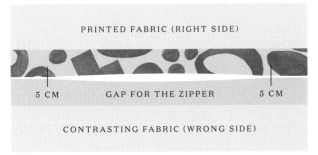

PRINTED FABRIC (RIGHT SIDE)

5 CM   GAP FOR THE ZIPPER   5 CM

CONTRASTING FABRIC (WRONG SIDE)

STEP 11

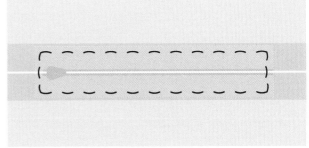

Running stitch diagram

Running stitch is the simplest of all the embroidery stitches and is also the most basic darning stitch. Bring your needle from the back of your work to the front. Move your needle over a stitch length and bring your needle from the front to the back – this makes one stitch. Leave a small gap before bringing your needle from the back to the front again. Repeat, trying to keep your stitches evenly sized and evenly spaced. When filling a space with running stitch, try to stagger your stitches in one line to fill the gaps in the next line, much like a brick pattern. When you are more confident, you can play with varying your stitches with long and short stitches.

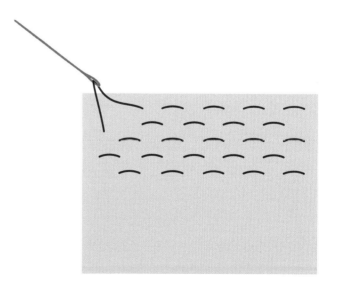

Templates

While ultimately, I would like you to create your own designs, these templates are a great starting point. For the stamp designs, use tracing paper to copy the designs and then transfer them to your carving material. For the lantern, photocopy the template then cut out to use as a template that you can draw around onto your cardboard. Have fun!

SENTIMENT TEMPLATE FOR MASKED GREETING CARD (PAGE 56)

FLOWER TEMPLATE FOR HAND-STAMPED DRINK COASTERS (PAGE 90)

LIPSTICK TEMPLATE FOR SPOT COLOUR COSMETICS POUCH (PAGE 104)

FLOWER TEMPLATES FOR MASKED
GREETING CARD (PAGE 56)

FLOWER TEMPLATE
FOR PAPER LANTERN
(PAGE 86)

FLOWER TEMPLATE
FOR BEESWAX
WRAPS (PAGE 98)

LANTERN TEMPLATE
FOR PAPER LANTERN (PAGE 86)
(NOTE: CUT TWO)

Resources

I would like to acknowledge that the printmaking community is a generous one, and I stand on the shoulders of giants. Over the years, I have worked with, learnt from and been inspired by many wonderful printmakers. If you are keen to pursue block printing further, I urge you to enrich your knowledge with the following resources:

Books

Balzer, Julie Fei Fan (2013), *Carve, Stamp, Play: Designing and Creating Custom Stamps*, Interweave Press, USA

Howard, Emily Louise (2019), *Block Print Magic*, Rockport Publishers, Beverly, MA

Lauren, Andrea (2016), *Block Print: Everything You Need to Know for Printing with Lino Blocks, Rubber Blocks, Foam Sheets, and Stamp Sets*, Rockport Publishers, Beverly, MA

Websites

Handprinted Blog – this is a wonderful resource, featuring many projects and techniques as well as a rundown of products and artist introductions. handprinted.co.uk/blogs/blog

LinocutBoy – Another wonderful and informative blog by the artist Nick Morley (A.K.A. Linocut Boy). Nick has some great information and tutorials specifically relating to lino cutting if that is something you would like to know more about. linocutboy.com/blog

Instagram

For more wonderful patterns, follow @regnitzflimmern

For amazing tessellations, check out @martaharveyart

If you need inspiration or enjoy the discipline of a daily challenge, I highly recommend some of these Instagram challenges:

#CarveDecember – hosted by @balzerdesigns, the challenge is to carve a stamp every day of December

#Inktober or #PrintInktober – either design or print something every day of October

#PrinterSolstice/@printersolstice – running from late December to early March, this is a weekly prompt-based printmaking challenge

#100DaysProject – set your own project (100 days of patterns?) and do it for 100 consecutive days

Acknowledgements

To put out a book on block printing is not something I would have been brave enough to consider by myself, so a big thanks to Kajal for taking a chance on me.

There are so many printmakers out there that inspire me but my biggest thanks goes to Julie Balzer. Her book and her yearly #CarveDecember challenge changed the way I approached block printing for the better, and she is not only a fabulous artist, but is also a generous, funny and kind human.

To all the people who have signed up to my workshops in the past – I have learnt as much from you as you have from me and I'm a better teacher because of you.

My creative community is dear to me and so important in terms of advice and encouragement. Thank you to the team of Sydney Made, Renee and Ange of D'Alton Baker Productions, Heidi Helyard, Stephanie and Amy of Outer Island and Mia of Ruby Raisin. I owe a massive shout out to Samee Lapham and Claire Cassidy for making the photoshoot such a fun, creative and enriching experience.

To my family back in Aotearoa, thank you for giving me a strong creative foundation, and to my family-in-law across the Pacific, thank you for putting your hands up to buy the first copies!

A big thank you to my mother-in-law, who did a mountain of work keeping my household running while I had my head down trying to write.

To my bright and beautiful daughters, who tell me daily that they believe in me. I hope this book makes up for all the ways in which I embarrass you. This book is for you.

Finally, I owe a debt of gratitude to my darling Ben who, since the day I said 'I want to make art my day job' has supported this big dream of mine. Love you long time, hubby.

About the author

Rowan Sivyer, A.K.A. Little Rowan Redhead, is a self-taught printmaker, illustrator and painter (as well as a self-confessed hobby hoarder and compulsive maker). She draws most of her inspiration from the native flora and fauna of her adopted country, Australia, and her native country, New Zealand. Rowan paints, carves or prints every day. She is fuelled by a creative curiosity that has been with her from childhood, passed on from creative parents. This hasn't always been Rowan's day job – she has a PhD in International Relations. However, a family health scare in 2012 was a watershed moment that put Rowan on the path to becoming a full-time artist.

Her thirst for new techniques has led her down many paths: acrylics, collage, screen printing and stitching are just a few examples. However, Rowan has an 'enduring crush' on block printing that has been with her since high school (even ramming a lino cutter into her hand didn't put her off!). Rowan began teaching block printing in 2017 and loves sharing her passion with others. The best part of the job is the 'aha' moments her students have when they print their first stamp.

Rowan lives on beautiful Gadigal Country in Sydney, Australia, with her husband Ben, two daughters, Stella and Audrey, and two rambunctious dogs, Chilli and Pepper.

You can find more of Rowan's work at www.littlerowanredhead.com, on Instagram @littlerowanredhead or on TikTok.

Index

A

acrylic paint 16
air-dry clay Christmas ornaments
94–7

B

bags
*foam-printed reversible planter
bag* 110–15
potato-printed tote bag 78–81
spot colour cosmetics zip pouch
104–9
upcycled grocery bags 66
barens 17
beeswax wraps: *hand-printed
beeswax wraps* 98–103
blocks. *see also stamps*
cleaning 31
grouping 46
lining up 41
multi-colour 35
placement of 30
preparing 26
spot colour 32
brayers 16, 30
bunting: *party polka dots!* 82–5
burnishing paper 17, 30

C

cake toppers: *party polka dots!*
82–5
carbon paper 26
card
masked greeting card 56–9
upcycled card gift tags 60–3
carving 28
carving tools 13
holding 13, 28
maintenance 14
Christmas: *air-dry clay Christmas
ornaments* 94–7
clay: *air-dry clay Christmas
ornaments* 94–7
cleaning blocks 31
coasters: *hand-stamped drink
coasters* 90–3
collages: *print collage still life* 74–7
colour
contrast 46
ghost printing 38
jigsaw printing 39
multi-colour blocks 35
overprinting 36–7
print layering 36–7
spot colour blocks 32
colourful deli or tissue paper 67
contrast 46
cosmetics zip pouch: *spot colour
cosmetics zip pouch* 104–9
craft knives 14
cushions: *print and stitch cushion*
126–31

D

deli paper 17
colourful deli or tissue paper 67
paper lantern 86–9
designing stamps 22–3
drum lampshade 116–21

E

embroidery: *print and stitch
cushion* 126–31
envelopes 59

F

fabric 17
drum lampshade 116–21
*foam-printed reversible planter
bag* 110–15
furoshiki – fabric gift wrap 66
hand-printed beeswax wraps
98–103
print and stitch cushion 126–31
spot colour cosmetics zip pouch
104–9
fabric ink 16
foam-printed reversible planter bag
110–15
foam printing 21
foam stamps 21
fruit, printing with 20
furoshiki – fabric gift wrap 66

Published in 2022 by Hardie Grant Books,
an imprint of Hardie Grant Publishing

Hardie Grant Books (London)
5th & 6th Floors
52–54 Southwark Street
London SE1 1UN

Hardie Grant Books (Melbourne)
Building 1, 658 Church Street
Richmond, Victoria 3121

hardiegrantbooks.com

British Library Cataloguing-in-Publication Data. A catalogue record for this book is available
from the British Library.

Modern Block Printing
ISBN: 978-1-78488-518-2

10 9 8 7 6 5 4 3 2 1

Publishing Director: Kajal Mistry
Acting Publishing Director: Emma Hopkin
Editor: Eila Purvis
Designer: Studio Noel
Illustrations: Studio Noel
Photographer: Samee Lapham
Prop stylist: Claire Cassidy
Copy-editor: Marie Clayton
Proofreader: Tara O'Sullivan
Indexer: Cathy Heath
Production Controller: Sabeena Atchia

Colour reproduction by p2d
Printed and bound in China by Leo Paper Products Ltd.